This book belongs to:

"Colors! Colors! Where can you be?

Why are you totally hiding from me?

Mommy told me to look all around,

but who are you and where can you be found?"

"We are over here," they say.

"We are colors and we are coming your way.

Let us come and say hi.

We are the colors you are trying to spy."

4

"I am red! I sleep on your bed."

6

"I am blue! I go on your shoe."

8

"I am yellow! I am a bright and friendly fellow."

10

"But wait there is more..."

"Purple, orange, and green

are waving by the closet door."

"So as you can see,

we are all around you DLee."

16

"Now close your eyes and get ready for bed.

We will see you in the morning, sleepy head!"

18

If you liked this book, check out DLee in:

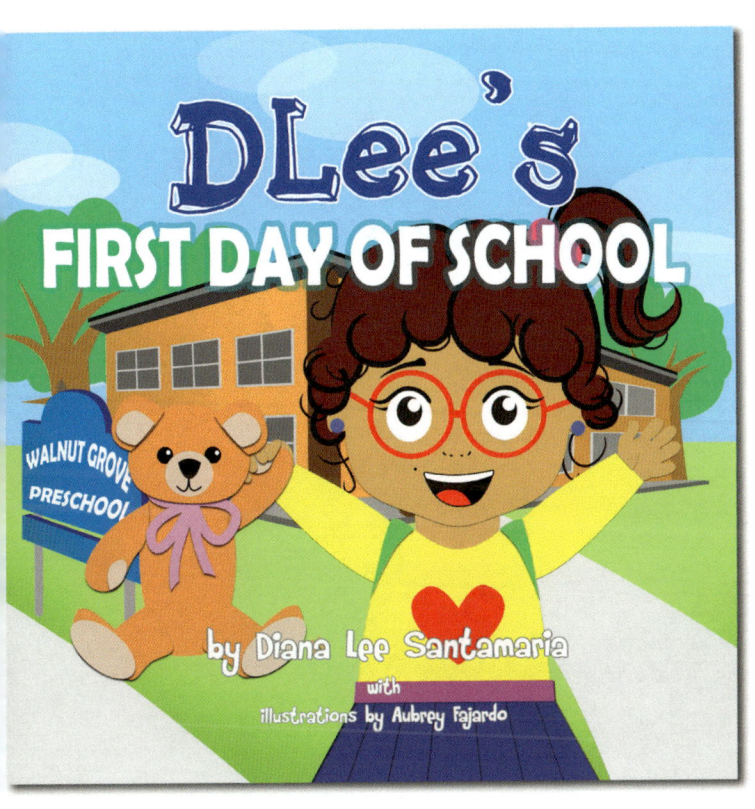

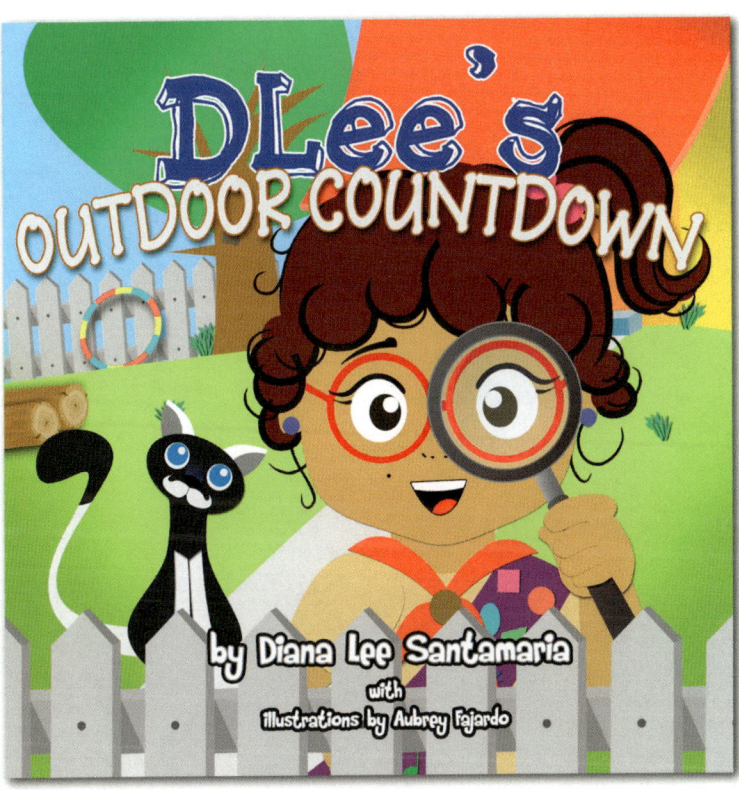

www.dleesworld.com

To Mia,

Thank you for being an excellent listener. Hope you enjoy reading the book at home!! :)

Nina Lee ♡

Made in the USA
Charleston, SC
06 September 2014